D0116204

Lauber, Patricia.
Who discovered America? :
mysteries and puzzles of
(New ed.) c1992

8/96

DATE DUE

JAN 02 1998		
NOV 19 1998		
DEC 05 1998		
DEC 18 1998		
NOV 15		
JUN 04 2002		
OCT 23		
DEC 18		
JAN 07 2003		
JAN 28 2003		

DEMCO 38-297

7/96

SOLANGE BUNICH

Who Discovered America?

MYSTERIES AND PUZZLES
OF THE NEW WORLD

NEW EDITION

Patricia Lauber

illustrated by Mike Eagle

HarperCollins*Publishers*

Also by Patricia Lauber

GET READY FOR ROBOTS!

HOW WE LEARNED THE EARTH IS ROUND

AN OCTOPUS IS AMAZING

SNAKES ARE HUNTERS

TALES MUMMIES TELL

VOYAGERS FROM SPACE: METEORS AND METEORITES

WHAT BIG TEETH YOU HAVE!

This book is based on an earlier one by Patricia Lauber,
WHO DISCOVERED AMERICA? (Random House, 1970)

Who Discovered America?: Mysteries and Puzzles of the New World
Text copyright © 1970, 1992 by Patricia G. Lauber
Illustrations copyright © 1992 by Mike Eagle

Library of Congress Cataloging-in-Publication Data
Lauber, Patricia.
   Who discovered America? : mysteries and puzzles of the New World /
by Patricia Lauber ; illustrated by Mike Eagle. — New ed.
       p.   cm.
   Includes index.
   Summary: Discusses how information on the settling and exploration
of America before Columbus has been compiled from archaeological
discoveries.
   ISBN 0-06-023728-7. — ISBN 0-06-023729-5 (lib. bdg.)
   1. America—Antiquities—Juvenile literature.   2. America—
Discovery and exploration—Pre-Columbian—Juvenile literature.
[1. America—Antiquities.   2. America—Discovery and exploration.
3. Archaeology.]   I. Eagle, Mike, ill.   II. Title.
E21.5.L38   1992
973.1'1—dc20   90-43604
                                                         CIP
                                                         AC

Contents

A Puzzling Discovery   5

The First Americans   15

Travelers from Afar?   27

Vinland the Good   39

The Clues to Vinland   53

Figures in the Mists   61

Who Discovered America?   71

For Further Reading   75

Index   77

A Puzzling Discovery

His name was Christopher Columbus, and he was a sailor with a bold plan. He would sail west from Europe, west across the Ocean Sea, west to the lands of Asia called the Indies. He would find a sea route to the pearls, gold, spices, silks, and perfumes of the Indies. For years traders had carried these riches overland to Europe. Now, with land routes closed by war, trade had stopped. Fame and fortune awaited the man who opened up a sea route.

The idea burned in him like a fever. He studied maps and read geography books. He sought advice from experts. He planned. And when he was ready, he began the search for backing, for money to make the trip. Finally he found a backer in Isabella, Queen of Spain.

And so it happened that on the morning of August 3, 1492, three small ships sailed from Palos, Spain. Their names were the *Niña*, the *Pinta*, and the *Santa María*. Aboard them were some ninety men, under the command of Columbus. As the ships cleared harbor, an ocean breeze filled their sails. The tiny fleet of ships surged forward, heading west.

But the voyage was not yet really under way. On the third day out, the *Pinta*'s rudder broke. The fleet was forced to stop at the Canary Islands for repairs. At last, on September 6, all was again ready. Once more the three small ships set out to sea.

At first the winds were light, sometimes dying altogether. For a few days the men could still see the mountain peaks of the Canary Islands. Then, on the evening of September 9, the last trace of land disappeared. Only the sea and the sky remained. Now the voyage had truly begun. They were sailing into the unknown.

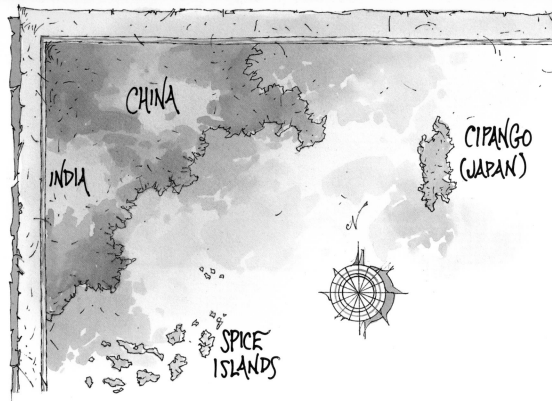

In his cabin Columbus had a chart that he had drawn himself. Like the best maps of his day, it showed a world much smaller than the one we know. And in this world the only known lands were Europe, Asia, and Africa. Together they formed a giant island surrounded by the Ocean Sea. Columbus's chart showed that Japan was the closest part of the Indies. It appeared as an island that lay only three thousand miles away. A month of sailing west should bring him to its pearls and gold.

For days, then weeks, they sailed across the empty

THE OCEAN SEA

IRELAND

AZORES

SPAIN EUROPE

CANARIES

CAPE VERDE ISLANDS

AFRICA

MAP of COLUMBUS'S TIME

ocean. They saw no land, not even an island. They saw no other sails. There was only the ocean, stretching on and on.

Each day Columbus wrote down how far he thought they had sailed. But he kept this record secret and gave a smaller figure to his men. He did not want them frightened by the distance they had sailed from home. Still, by early October everyone realized that they had sailed too far and too long. The men were restless and fearful. Columbus himself must have felt the touch of fear. He knew they had sailed far beyond the place where his map showed Japan. Had they somehow missed the island? If so, where were they now?

On October 7 the sky grew dark with the wings of birds. They were land birds, flying southwest. Columbus decided to follow the birds. During the next three days, huge flights of land birds passed overhead. The sight cheered the men, but even so they had had enough. By October 10 they had not seen land for thirty-one days. They demanded that Columbus turn back.

To have come so far, to be so close to land— Columbus could not turn back. He had come to find the Indies and he would find them. The men agreed to sail on for three more days.

The next day they found signs of land life floating in the sea: branches with leaves and berries, a hand-carved wooden pole, still more branches.

At two o'clock the following morning, the *Pinta*'s lookout cried, "*Tierra! Tierra!*" Land!

When daylight came, they saw they had reached a small island. Sailing around it, they found a bay, where they could anchor. Columbus named the island San Salvador and claimed it for Spain. The date was October 12, 1492.

There were people on the island. This did not surprise Columbus, because he expected to meet people in the Indies. What did surprise him about the Indians, as he called them, was the way they looked. He had expected to find people in silken robes. These wore no clothes at all and painted their faces, noses, or whole bodies. They were gentle people, though, and Columbus easily made friends with them. Soon the islanders were trading parrots and cotton yarn for tiny bells and glass beads.

Through sign language Columbus learned that there were many other islands to the south and west. He decided to sail on in search of Japan or China.

As everyone knows today, Columbus never reached the Indies. He had landed on one of the islands we call the Bahamas. Japan and China lay thousands of miles farther west, beyond a whole continent, beyond a second, bigger ocean. Yet Columbus's first and later voyages were important,

for they led to a great age of discovery.

As other men studied the plants, animals, and Indians that Columbus brought back, a mystery took shape: Where had Columbus been? Clearly it was not the Indies. Other explorers set sail to find out. After a while, the mystery was solved. Columbus had found a new world, later named the Americas.

But as this mystery was being solved, another was growing. Who were the Indians? Who were the people already living in the New World? In discovering the Americas, Columbus and other explorers had also discovered people who were completely unknown to Europeans.

The First Americans

The mystery of the Indians grew bigger and bigger as Europeans explored the Americas. For one thing, there were a great many Indians and they were spread over two whole continents, from the far north to the tip of South America. For another, the great many Indians lived in a great many different ways.

When he first landed in the New World, Columbus met timid, gentle Indians who were fishermen. On nearby islands, the Indians were warriors and cannibals. Later explorers of North America found tribes of Indians in the Southwest

15

PLAINS INDIAN

who lived year-round in large villages. These Indians were farmers who irrigated their fields. They were artists and craftsmen. On the Great Plains, Indians hunted bison with bows and arrows, traveling with the herd and living in tepees. In other areas of North America, small groups of Indians lived by gathering food—bulbs, roots, seeds, fruits, grasshoppers, nuts. Indians of the eastern woodlands lived by hunting, fishing, and farming.

16

The most surprising discoveries were the great civilizations of the Aztecs, the Mayas, and the Incas.

The Aztecs, of central Mexico, were engineers, builders, painters, sculptors, and craftsmen. They had built a great city, with palaces of stone and temples shaped like pyramids. They had built islands in lakes as places to grow food. They had developed a kind of writing that used signs and pictures, knew much about astronomy, and had invented a calendar.

In southern Mexico and Guatemala, Europeans found the ruins of a once-great civilization. Here the

AZTECS

Mayas had built stone temples and laid out paved roads. They had built raised roads across wet ground. They had been skilled in art, astronomy, and mathematics.

The Incas of Peru were builders of cities, roads, and bridges. They were farmers who made terraces on mountainsides to hold the soil in place and who irrigated desert land along the coast. They raised animals for meat and wool. Craftsmen wove fine cloth and made pottery. They used gold, silver, tin, and copper to make jewelry and sculpture. The Incas governed an empire that was nearly three thousand miles long and held perhaps sixteen million people. It was bigger than any kingdom of Europe.

MAYAS

Scholars and other men of learning were greatly puzzled. Who were the Indians? Had they always lived in the New World? If not, where had they come from? Could the Aztecs, Mayas, and Incas have developed their great civilizations without help from the Old World? Perhaps the earliest settlers had been colonists or shipwrecked sailors from ancient Egypt or Greece. Or perhaps they were Romans or Phoenicians. But if that was so, then who were the other Indians? It was a baffling mystery.

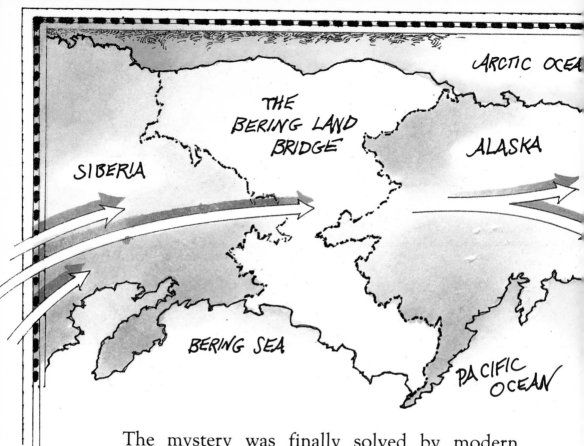

The mystery was finally solved by modern scientists. They have discovered that the first Americans came from Siberia thousands of years ago. They arrived during the Ice Age, a time when huge sheets of ice covered large parts of northern lands.

The ice was made of water from the seas. As the sun's heat drew moisture into the air, clouds formed. Rain and snow fell. Where the snow fell on northern lands, it did not melt away in summer. Instead, it piled up for hundreds or thousands of

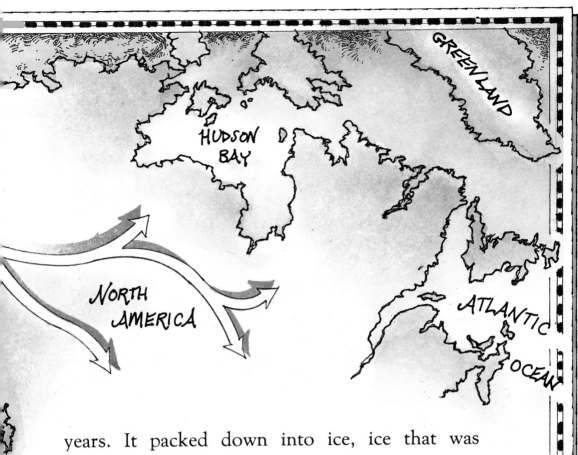

years. It packed down into ice, ice that was sometimes a mile or more thick.

Because all this water was locked up on land as ice, sea levels fell. At the height of the Ice Age, sea levels were three hundred feet lower than they are at present. Large areas now under water were then dry land.

Today water separates Siberia and Alaska. During the Ice Age the water disappeared. The sea bottom became a wide plain. It formed a bridge of land between Siberia and Alaska.

Perhaps one day a small band of people—men, women, and children—set out in search of game. The hunt led them onto a rolling plain that was free of ice. In the days that followed, the people went on moving eastward across the plain. In time they came to a different place, where the hunting was excellent. They stayed on in what is now Alaska and so became the first people ever to set foot in the Americas. They were followed by other bands of hunters. There were times when an ice-free route opened up, leading south. People moved on, into the eastern Rocky Mountains and the Great Plains.

Or perhaps the first settlers of North America followed the southern coast of the land bridge, fishing and hunting mammals of the sea. And in time they came to a new land, where they stayed.

We may never know just how or when the first settlers crossed that bridge. Any clues they left behind are now buried at the bottom of the sea. But we do know that in time the descendants of these people settled the Americas and became the Indians that Columbus and other explorers met.

We also have many clues to how these early settlers lived. The clues have been found by archeologists, scientists who dig up traces of ancient peoples and civilizations. Usually they find the most recent traces of people near the surface. As they dig down, they keep finding older and older clues to people who once lived in a place. Often they can date the clues. By analyzing a piece of charcoal, for example, they may be able to tell how long ago a tree died and was turned into firewood.

Archeologists may find tools, weapons, charcoal

from ancient campfires, and bones that have been cooked. These are signs of a people who lived by hunting, who cooked and ate meat. The bones tell what kinds of animals they hunted and ate. Scraping tools and needles tell that they used hides to make clothing and perhaps shelter. Fishhooks and scraps of net tell of a people who fished. Bits of pottery tell whether people were just starting to make pottery or were skilled at it. Archeologists may find jewelry made of seashells hundreds of miles from the sea. The jewelry tells them of trade between people who lived inland and people who lived by the sea.

Sometimes archeologists find a place where people lived for hundreds of years. Here they can see how life changed as the people made discoveries and inventions. Perhaps at first the people hunted small animals and deer and took fish, shellfish, and turtles from a nearby river. Later they had milling and grinding stones, a sign that they were now eating seeds, nuts, and roots. They had also developed better hunting weapons. Still later they learned to raise food crops and to make pottery and baskets.

Once people learn to farm, they have a year-round supply of food. They do not need to spend all their time and energy hunting animals and gathering plant food. They have time to develop arts and crafts, religions, governments—to build a civilization. And that, many archeologists believe, was how the great civilizations of the Aztecs, the Mayas, and the Incas developed. The Indians did not have to have help from the Old World.

Yet archeologists have also found signs that some Indians met travelers from other lands long before Columbus arrived in the Bahamas.

Travelers from Afar?

Some time ago an odd rock was found on the coast of Maine. There was lettering on it. The carved letters were weathered but could still be read. They spelled out a few lines from a famous Latin poem, the *Aeneid*.

To some people the rock was proof that a Roman ship had been wrecked on the coast of Maine. They imagined sailors carving the rock to leave a sign of themselves.

To scientists the carving is not proof of anything. It looks old, but there is no way of telling whether it was carved two hundred or two thousand years ago.

The lines are in Latin, but they are from a poem studied in schools everywhere. The rock tells us only that at some unknown time some unknown person carved a few lines of Latin on it.

Archeologists would be pleased to find a clue of this sort, if they could prove it was genuine. But they do not really expect to find written messages from ancient travelers. They look instead for ideas and objects that appear suddenly, that do not seem to grow out of other things that people were doing. And that is what some archeologists may have found near the fishing village of Valdivia, Ecuador.

They were digging up traces of people who lived some five thousand years ago. The people had been hunters, fishermen, and gatherers. They had simple stone tools for cutting, chopping, and scraping. They used pebbles as sinkers for their fishing lines, and they sawed fishhooks out of shells. Mixed in with the remains of shells, fishbones, and tools was some broken pottery.

At the time, it was the earliest pottery ever found in the New World. And it appeared suddenly in the

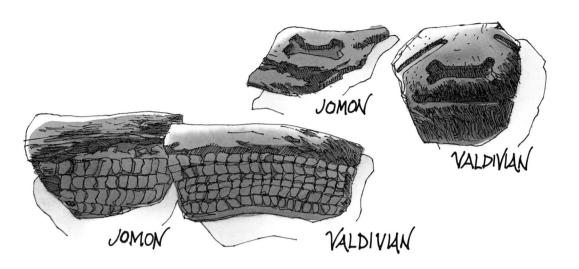

JOMON

VALDIVIAN

JOMON

VALDIVIAN

layers of tools and shells. The archeologists first thought that the people were probably just learning to make pottery. When they sorted the pieces, they got a big surprise. The pottery was the work of skilled craftsmen. Something else was even more surprising. The shapes and patterns were like those of Jomon pottery made five thousand years ago in southern Japan.

Some archeologists think there is only one way to explain the pottery. Jomon deep-sea fishermen were caught in a storm and blown out to sea. Their boat was seized by strong currents flowing east, and they could not make their way back to Japan. Like many island people today, the fishermen knew how to

29

keep themselves alive at sea in a small boat. They sailed on, carried by winds and currents, and landed in Ecuador. With them came pottery and a knowledge of how to make it.

Other archeologists think the pottery was made by the people who lived near Valdivia. Skilled pottery making appears suddenly, they say, only because no one has found earlier pottery. But whatever the truth may be, there are other signs of visitors from Asia in the same region.

Digging north of Valdivia, archeologists came on a strange group of pottery objects. All the objects were common in Asia. None have been found anywhere else in the New World. These tell of a possible visit to Ecuador by travelers from Asia about two thousand years ago.

Some of the objects were pottery models of houses. They are the kinds of houses that were built in Southeast Asia but not in the New World. There were little seated figures with folded legs. They look like the little pottery figures made in India and other Asian countries. There were pottery ear-

SOUTH
AMERICA

NORTH AMERICA

ALASKA

NORTH
PACIFIC OCEAN

ALEUTIAN
ISLANDS

BERING
SEA

HAWAIIAN ISLANDS

This map, which has east at the top, shows the North Pacific as Asians thought of it. It is possible to follow the coastline from Asia to the New World. If ancient travelers reached the new world, they probably took such a route, rather than sailing across the Pacific.

SIBERIA

E

N

S

JAPAN

CHINA

W

OLD WORLD

NEW WORLD

plugs shaped like golf tees, just like the ones used in Japan. There were pottery neck rests, the kind widely used in Egypt, India, China, and other parts of the Old World.

All these objects appear suddenly in Ecuador. They do not seem related to other New World pottery, but they are like pottery of the Old World. Archeologists think that the ideas for them must have come from Asia.

There are other hints of ancient visitors from Asia. One is the game we call Parcheesi. The same game with the same rules was played by Asians and by Indians of Mexico. How could the game have reached the New World unless it traveled with people?

Some ancient art of Middle America is strangely like ancient art of Southeast Asia. Both show strong men carrying heavy objects on their shoulders. They show tiger thrones and seated lions, although there were no tigers and lions in the New World. They show diving gods and gods standing on crouched human figures.

If the art of Southeast Asia traveled to the Americas, it must have come on ships. And ancient records do tell of ships that could have crossed the Pacific. Some seventeen hundred years ago, both China and India had colonies in other parts of Asia. Goods traveled back and forth on ships that could carry six hundred people and more than a thousand tons of cargo.

The travel diary of a Chinese man tells of his return home from India. He sailed on a large ship that carried more than two hundred sailors and passengers. During a big storm, the ship was damaged. It drifted for ninety days, finally reaching Java. There the traveler took passage on another ship of the same size. It set out on a fifty-day run to Canton, China. But because of storms the trip took eighty-two days.

Both of these were large ships, which could feed some two hundred people for three months. Such ships could have crossed the Pacific, perhaps first by chance, then later on purpose.

No known records tell of such voyages. But the finds of pottery and art make many archeologists think that Asians did visit the New World a number of times. Then, for some reason, they stopped.

When there is no written history, it is hard to look back through time. It is like trying to see through mist or fog. You see a large dark shape but you cannot tell if it is a cow or a car. Archeologists look back through time and see what appear to be travelers from Asia, but the mists are thick.

A few other shapes are even harder to make out. Here the clues are not pottery and art but stories— Indian myths and legends. They tell of bearded, fair-skinned gods who lived among the Indians from Brazil to Peru to Mexico. The gods taught them many things, then sailed away across the ocean.

When the Spanish conquerors arrived, the Indians at first thought the bearded gods had returned. They were slow to understand, slow to see the need to defend themselves.

Legends alone are not proof that Europeans visited the Indians. Yet there is one clue that does suggest visitors from northern Europe. It is found in Spanish accounts of the Inca empire. These say that most of the Indians were small and dark. But members of the ruling family were tall and fair-skinned, and some had red hair.

No one may ever find out if northern Europeans reached South America and became the gods of Indian legend. But we do know that some twelve hundred years ago they were reaching out across the

North Atlantic. Vikings—men and women from Scandinavia—settled Iceland and Greenland. And then they went on to explore the place they called Vinland the Good.

Vinland the Good

Much of what we know about the Vikings comes from the stories called sagas. The sagas were tales of Viking history. They were told aloud and passed on from one generation to the next. They were first written down about eight hundred years ago.

Sagas tell us that the Viking discovery of Iceland took place around the year 860. The discoverers were sailors who were blown far off course by storms and so came to Iceland. The first Viking settlers arrived in 874 and were soon followed by others. By the year 930, between twenty thousand and thirty thousand settlers were living in Iceland.

The land was not good for farming, but it had pastures where the settlers raised sheep and cattle. Fishing was excellent. There were birds to hunt and eggs to collect. There were seals in the harbor. Icelanders carried on trade with Norway, Ireland, and England.

One of the Icelanders was named Eric the Red, for the color of his hair. In 982 Eric took part in an outbreak of killings. As punishment, he was forced to leave Iceland for three years. He decided to explore a land to the west that had been sighted earlier. He spent the next three years sailing along its coasts and exploring. Most of the land was covered by a huge ice cap. But on the western coast he found two good green strips of land. There were animals that could be hunted. The sea was full of fish, seals, and walruses. Summers on the west coast were short but pleasant, and the pastures were sheltered by low hills. Best of all, he saw no people. The land was his for the taking. He decided to settle it.

Eric returned to Iceland and told of the new land. To attract settlers, he called it Greenland. Within a few years between two thousand and three thousand people had left Iceland and settled there.

A saga tells us that in the summer of 986 a shipowner named Bjarni Herjolfsson was sailing from Iceland to Greenland to visit his father. He had never sailed these waters before, but he was sure he would recognize the snow-covered mountains of Greenland when he saw them.

Three days out of Iceland, the ship was driven south by winds and then ran into fog. The ship drifted and drifted through the fog. Bjarni and his crew had no idea where they were. When the sun at last broke through, they spread their sails and soon sighted a land of forests and low hills. Whatever this was, Bjarni knew it was not Greenland. So he turned north and sailed along the coast for two days. Now the land was wooded but flat. Another three days' sailing brought them to a place that was covered with mountains and glaciers and flat stones. To Bjarni this did not look like Greenland either, so he sailed on to the east. In four days' time he came to Greenland. There he settled with his father and gave up voyaging.

Because he was eager to reach Greenland, Bjarni had not stopped to explore the lands he had sighted. And in Greenland, people were busy settling a new land. Fifteen years passed before anyone set out to explore the new lands to the west. The person who did was Leif Ericsson, son of Eric the Red.

Leif bought Bjarni's ship and gathered a crew. He expected his father to take charge of the voyage, but as he was riding down to the ship, Eric fell off his horse and was injured. Leif took command of the ship and sailed west.

He came first to a barren land with not even a blade of grass. Inland the ground was covered by great glaciers. Between the glaciers and the sea, the land was like one flat rock. Leif named the place Helluland, meaning Flatstone Land, and sailed on.

The second land Leif and his men came to was low-lying and wooded. It had wide beaches of white sand that sloped gently into the sea. Leif named this place Markland, meaning Woodland, and again sailed on.

Two days later they sighted a third land. They first went ashore on an island, where the grass was sweet with dew. Then they sailed behind the island and up a river, where they anchored. They unloaded the ship and built shelters with tree branches.

Leif soon decided to build houses here and spend

the winter. This was fine country. There was plenty of fish and game. There was grass, and the climate seemed so mild that their cattle could graze all winter. He also sent out scouting parties to explore the land. One evening a German member of the crew came back greatly excited. He had found grapevines and grapes, things he knew well, because they grew in his homeland. When Leif sailed back to Greenland, he took a cargo of timber, grapevines, and grapes. He gave the name Vinland to the place where he had wintered. It meant Grapeland or Wineland, and it became known as Vinland the Good.

The next voyage to Vinland was made by Leif's brother Thorvald, who spent the winter at Leif's camp. In spring and summer, some of the men explored to the west, where they found woods, beaches, and islands. They saw no signs of people except for a wooden building on an island, in which grain was stored.

The second summer Thorvald sailed east and north. He found a wooded, high point of land. It was

so beautiful that he wanted to build his house there. When the men went ashore, they saw three skin boats. Under each of the boats were three men. They were Skraelings, a name the sagas use for both Eskimos and Indians. Thorvald and his men set upon the Skraelings and killed all except one, who escaped in a boat. By morning, the Greenlanders found themselves under attack by countless Skraelings in skin boats. Thorvald was wounded by an arrow and died. He was buried on the land where he had wished to live.

Neither Leif nor Thorvald had tried to start a colony in Vinland. But another voyager soon did. He was an Icelander named Thorfinn Karlsefni, who had sailed to Greenland and stayed on. He married Gudrid, the widow of one of Eric's sons. Karlsefni and Gudrid set out with a party of sixty men, five women, and all kinds of livestock. They landed at Leif's camp, where the men spent much of their time cutting timber.

In summer Skraelings appeared out of the woods, carrying bundles of furs. They wished to trade the

furs for weapons, but Karlesfni traded milk instead. Early in the second winter the Skraelings returned, again bringing furs for trade. But this time one of them tried to steal some weapons. A fight broke out and a number of Skraelings were killed. Karlsefni decided that the dangers of Vinland were too great for a small colony. The following spring he loaded his ship with furs, timbers, and grapes and returned to Greenland. The saga ends by telling of the good life that Karlsefni and Gudrid later lived in Iceland.

The dates in the saga are not clear. But the voyages to Vinland seem to have taken place between the years 1000 and 1020. It is clear, though, that Vinland the Good lay west of Greenland and was a land where trees grew tall, grapes grew wild, and cattle could graze all winter. If the saga is true, this pleasant land must have been part of North America.

There are many reasons for thinking that the saga is true. One has to do with peoples who have no written history. The only way they can know their past is to tell truly what happened. The tellers of stories have a duty to tell the truth. Perhaps small changes creep into a story during hundreds of tellings, but the main story stays true.

A second reason is that the discovery of Vinland was known to a number of people outside Greenland. Vinland is mentioned, for example, in a world geography written by a German named Adam of Bremen around 1075. Adam had spent some time with Svein, king of the Danes, asking about voyages in the northern seas. From Svein he learned of a place called Vinland, which had been discovered in the ocean and visited a number of times. It was famous for its wild grapes. Vinland was also mentioned in the *Book of Icelanders*, written by Ari Thorgilsson around 1121. Ari did not describe Vinland but simply mentioned it. He seemed to think that it was a place that everyone knew about.

The findings of archeologists are another reason for thinking that the sagas are true. For example, sagas tell us that all his life Eric the Red was faithful to the gods worshipped by early peoples of the north. But his son Leif became a Christian while on a visit to Norway. Leif preached Christianity on his return, and one of the first people to change beliefs was his mother. She built the first Christian church in Greenland. Archeologists have found the remains of that church a few hundred yards from the remains of Leif's house.

But there is one big question the sagas do not answer: Where in North America was Vinland?

The Clues to Vinland

The visits to Vinland were made nearly a thousand years ago. They were made by small groups of people who stayed only a short time. There cannot be many traces of the visits. Yet the area where they might be found is huge.

Most of the people who have tried to find Vinland started with the stories of the Viking voyages. They looked for places that matched ones in the sagas. They came to think that the land of mountains, glaciers, and flat stone must be the southern part of Baffin Island. If so, then Markland, named for its woods, must be Labrador. And the next place that Leif came to—Vinland—must be Newfoundland.

To us Newfoundland does not seem much like Vinland the Good. It is a chilly, rather barren island. To people from Greenland it may have looked very different. They were not farmers looking for farmland. They were hunters, fishermen, and keepers of livestock. They were also men from an Arctic land without trees. Newfoundland may have seemed good beyond their dreams. There was game to be hunted and fish to be caught. There were great forests of spruce, balsam, fir, and birch. The climate was much milder than Greenland's. And the earth held something else they needed—iron ore for making tools and weapons.

There is another reason for linking Newfoundland with Vinland. Sailing south, an explorer must make a choice when he reaches Newfoundland. He must either turn east and sail along the island's Atlantic coast or turn west and sail between the island and the mainland.

A turning point is a likely place to build a base. It

CANADA   HUDSON BAY

EW
NGLAND

NOVA
SCOTIA

NWFOUNDLAND   LABRADOR

BAFFIN ISLAND

L'ANSE AUX
MEADOWS

GREENLAND

ARCTIC
OCEAN

ATLANTIC
OCEAN

ICELAND

IRELAND

SCANDINAVIA

SPAIN

EUROPE

This map looks west, showing the North
Atlantic as the Vikings thought of it.

is easy to find again—and Thorvald and Karlsefni were able to find Leif's camp with no trouble.

That is why two Norwegians, an explorer and his archeologist wife, decided to look for Leif's camp on the tip of Newfoundland. They began a search. Digging near the tiny fishing village of L'Anse aux Meadows in 1961, they came upon the ruins of an early settlement. They found traces of houses and a smithy, where bog iron was made into metal.

Not much is left of the houses—earth floors, the outlines of turf walls, and hearths. But the houses were built in the Viking style, which was also used in Greenland. The Indians and Eskimos did not build houses of this kind and did not know how to forge iron.

Besides the houses and smithy, a few small objects were found: some very rusty nails and pieces of iron, a small piece of copper, a stone lamp of the kind used in Iceland, a stone for sharpening needles, and a piece of bone needle. There was also a doughnut-shaped piece of soapstone. It was a spindle whorl, the kind used in Norway by women spinning wool.

Charcoal was found in the smithy and was later dated. It came from a tree that died around the time of the Viking trips to Vinland.

All these clues seem to say the same thing. This was a Viking settlement. And there is a good chance that it was the place where Leif built his houses.

Even so, there are ways in which Newfoundland does not seem like Vinland. For example, grapes do not grow wild in Newfoundland. And its Indians were the Beothuks, a shy people who were in no way warlike. They do not sound like the Skraelings the Vikings met. That is why many people now think

that Newfoundland was only one part of Vinland. They think it was the base from which the Vikings explored south. They think that Vinland started in Newfoundland and reached far south into New England.

Grapes do grow wild in New England. And the Skraelings sound like the Algonquin Indians of eastern North America. They were skilled hunters, trappers, and fishermen. Some tribes farmed, storing their corn in wooden buildings like the one discovered by Thorvald's men. Later settlers found the Algonquins friendly at first. The Indians often offered bundles of furs for trade or as gifts. But if trouble broke out, the Algonquins fought bravely and well.

There is still another reason to think that Vinland reached south into New England. This clue was found in Greenland, in the house where Karlsefni lived after his marriage to Gudrid. In one of the rooms archeologists came upon a lump of coal. The closest place to find this kind of coal is in Rhode Island. So it seems that Karlsefni may have sailed that far south. Like many other travelers, he picked up some souvenirs before returning home. One was a lump of coal.

The voyages of discovery came to an end, but Greenlanders went on sailing to Markland and Vinland for timber and furs, which they used in trade. New World products appear on Norwegian port records. Records in Iceland tell of a Greenland ship driven by storms into a harbor in western Iceland. The ship had been to Markland for timber.

Then the voyages stopped. Norway had lost interest in trading with Greenland. To make matters worse, the climate cooled and Greenland became much colder. By the middle 1500s the Greenlanders had disappeared. No one has ever known what became of them. Perhaps they simply died. Perhaps they were killed by Skraelings. Perhaps they packed up and sailed away. Whatever happened, they joined the many other figures hidden in the mists of time.

Figures in the Mists

The Vikings are the most famous early sailors of the North Atlantic. But other people in small boats also sailed that sea, both after the early Vikings and before. Traces of them appear in old books and records.

There is, for example, a geography book written by Dicuil, an Irish monk, around the year 825. In it he tells of some Irish priests who sailed to Iceland one winter in the late 700s and stayed for six months. It is clear from what Dicuil says that the priests were going to visit a place they knew about. They also knew the route and that winter was a good

time to make the trip. And if they went to Iceland in winter, they must have expected to find food and shelter there—to find a colony of priests, monks, and other people. That is, there were Irish settlers in Iceland long before the Vikings arrived.

Ari in the *Book of Icelanders* also tells of an Irish

settlement. He says there were Christian priests living in Iceland at the time the Vikings arrived. They later went away because they did not wish to live with people who worshipped false gods. They left behind bells, books, and other objects that showed they were Irish.

Perhaps the priests and the people who took care of them sailed back to Ireland. Perhaps they sailed west. They seem simply to have gone away—to have sailed out of the pages of history. Yet there is some reason to think that they—or other priests and monks—sailed west. The sagas tell us that when the

Vikings settled Greenland, they were surprised to find traces of an Irish settlement. The sagas also tell of a land to the west, near Vinland, a land of people who were Irish. There may or may not have been such a land. No one can be sure. For all we know, the Irish may have become the fair-skinned bearded gods of the Indians of South America.

Then there is the bishop who sailed out of the pages of history. Records in Iceland show that in 1112 the Pope made Eric Gnupsson "Bishop of Greenland and nearby islands." Around 1120 the bishop set out on a visit to Vinland. The records do not tell whether he reached Vinland or whether he ever returned to Greenland. If he did return, perhaps he wrote a report to the Pope that will someday be found.

By the time that trade was dying out between Greenland and Norway, other ships were sailing the northern waters. They were manned by fishermen from Bristol, England.

Bristol was one of England's leading ports. Trading ships often sailed between Bristol and Iceland. Bristol was also a place where many Norwegians had settled. Like other northern sailors, the men of Bristol knew about Vinland, knew there was land on the far side of the ocean. In the late 1400s, they began making some long and mysterious trips. Old records tell us that year after year they sailed west and were gone for many weeks. Some of the ships carried huge amounts of salt, and salt was used to preserve fish. Sometimes the ships were supposed to be going to Ireland, a short distance away. But they were gone for a long time. When they returned, they were not carrying salmon and linens from Ireland. They were carrying salt cod and hides.

Where had they been? The most likely answer is
Newfoundland. An area off Newfoundland, called
the Grand Banks, is one of the richest fishing
grounds in the world. Once discovered, it would
have been a secret well worth keeping.

Old records are one clue to where the fishermen
of Bristol were going. Another is a letter written by
a merchant of Bristol. It describes the first voyage of
an explorer named John Cabot.

Cabot was born in Genoa, now part of Italy, and his name at birth was Giovanni Caboto. Little is known about his life before he appeared in England in the late 1400s. He arrived with a globe of the world, which he had made himself, a map, and a plan to sail west to the Indies.

The place Cabot went in England was Bristol. The king granted Cabot the right to explore in the name of England. But it was the merchants of Bristol who gave Cabot the ships, sailors, and money that he needed.

On his first voyage, Cabot reached land in late June of 1497. The letter written by the merchant describes what Cabot saw, and so we know that the land must have been Newfoundland or Nova Scotia. It goes on to say that this land is believed to be the one found earlier by fishermen of Bristol.

Like Columbus, Cabot was sure that land on the far side of the ocean had to be Asia. On his second voyage, he planned to cross the ocean and then sail south until he reached the Indies. But we do not know how far he went. We do not know whether he ever understood that the land could not be Asia, for John Cabot never came back. In some unknown place, he went down with his ship. He became one more figure hidden by the mists of time. But England's claims in the New World started with Cabot. And his voyages helped lead the way to the European discovery of America.

Who Discovered America?

Over the years, many, many people arrived in the Americas. There were hunters from Siberia, perhaps fishermen and traders from Asia, and other ancient peoples. Irish priests and monks may have reached the Americas. The Vikings and fishermen of Bristol certainly did. And there may have been others we do not know about. But still, maps of the world went unchanged. Men of great learning went on believing that only an ocean lay between Europe and the Indies.

When Cabot set sail, he knew there was land

within reach. Columbus may also have known. As a young man he had sailed the northern seas as far as Iceland. It is possible that he had heard of Vinland and, like Cabot, believed it must be northeast Asia. Both set out thinking that they would find a sea route to the riches of the Indies.

Both were mistaken, yet their voyages touched off a great age of discovery and exploration. Before it ended, the map of the world was much changed. Two large continents and a big ocean were added to it.

Who discovered America? It is not an easy question to answer. But if someone asked you, what would you say?

For Further Reading/Index

For Further Reading

Bateman, Penny. *Aztecs and Incas*. New York: Franklin Watts, 1988.

Beck, Barbara L. *The Ancient Maya*. New York: Franklin Watts, 1988.

——— . *The Incas*. New York: Franklin Watts, 1983.

Clarke, Helen. *Vikings*. New York: Gloucester Press, 1979.

Fritz, Jean. *Where Do You Think You're Going, Christopher Columbus?* New York: Putnam, 1981.

Gallant, Roy A. *Ancient Indians: The First Americans*. New York: Enslow Publications, 1989.

Gibson, Michael. *The Vikings*. Englewood Cliffs, NJ: Silver Burdett, 1977.

Goodnough, David. *John Cabot and Son*. Mahwah, NJ: Troll Assocs., 1979.

Humble, Richard. *The Age of Leif Eriksson*. New York: Franklin Watts, 1989.

Meltzer, Milton. *Columbus and the World Around Him*. New York: Franklin Watts, 1990.

Odijik, Pamela. *The Aztecs*. Englewood Cliffs, NJ: Silver Burdett, 1990.

———. *The Maya.* Englewood Cliffs, NJ: Silver Burdett, 1990.

Roop, Peter and Connie, eds. *I, Columbus. My Journal—1492–3.* New York: Walker and Company, 1990.

Schiller, Barbara. *Eric the Red and Leif the Lucky.* Mahwah, NJ: Troll Assocs., 1979.

Stuart, Gene S. *The Mighty Aztecs.* Washington, DC: National Geographic Society, 1981.

Stuart, George E. and Gene S. Stuart. *The Mysterious Maya.* Washington, DC: National Geographic Society, 1977.

Wood, Marion. *Ancient America.* New York: Facts on File, 1990.

Index

Adam of Bremen, 51

Alaska and land bridge, 21, 23

Algonquins, 59

archeologists, how work, 24–26,
    28, 33, 52, 56–57

art of New World and Old World,
    33–34

Asia, possible visitors from, 28–34,
    36–37

Aztecs, 17, 26

Baffin Island, 53

Bahamas as landfall, 11

Beothuks, 57

Book of Icelanders, 51

Bristol, England, 65, 68
    fishermen, 65, 67

Cabot, John, 67–69, 71–72

Canary Islands, 6

China, ancient ships of, 34, 36

coal from Rhode Island, 59–60

Columbus, Christopher
    chart, 8
    first landfall, 10
    first voyage, 5–15
    importance of, 11, 15, 72
    people discovered, 11
    plan of, 5
    ships of, 6
    visit to Iceland, 72

Dicuil (Irish monk), 61

Ecuador, early pottery of, 28–30,
    33

Eric the Red, and discovery of
    Greenland, 42

Ericsson, Leif, and discovery of
    Vinland, 44–45, 56–57

Ericsson, Thorvald, voyages to
    Vinland, 45, 47

Europe, possible early visitors from, 37

First Americans
  arrival in Americas, 23
  ways of life, 23–26
  origins, 20
Flatstone Land. *See* Helluland.

gods, fair-skinned, of Indians, 37, 64
Gnupsson, Bishop Eric, 64–65
Greenland
  bishop of, 64–65
  discovery and settlement, 42–43
  end of settlement, 60
  first Christian church in, 52
  Irish settlement, 63–64
Guatemala, 17

Helluland, 44, 53
Herjolfsson, Bjarni, sighting of
    North America, 42–43

Ice Age
  causes of, 20–21
  defined, 20
  effect on oceans, 21
Iceland
  discovery and settlement, 39–40
  Irish colony, 61–63
  visit by Columbus, 72

Incas, 17–19, 26, 37
Indian civilizations, 17–19, 26
Indians, 37
  ancestors of, 20
  civilizations of, 17–19, 26
  and Columbus, 11, 15
  mystery of origins, 14–19
  mystery solved, 20–23
  ways of life, 15–19
Indies, the, 8, 11
  riches of, 5
  routes to, 5
Irish priests in Iceland, 61–63
Irish settlement in Greenland, 63–64
Irish settlements in Iceland, 62–63
iron ore, 54, 56
Isabella, Queen of Spain, 6

Japan, 8, 11, 29–30
  fishermen from, 29–30
  Jomon pottery, 29–30
  part of the Indies, 8, 11

Karlsefni, Thorfinn and Gudrid, 47, 50, 59–60

Labrador, 53
land bridge between Siberia and
    Alaska, 21
  as route to the Americas, 21, 23
L'Anse aux Meadows, 56–57, 59

Maine, 27
maps
   Bering land bridge, 20–21
   North Atlantic Ocean, 55
   North Pacific Ocean, 31
   world in the time of Columbus,
     8–9
Markland, 53, 60
Mayas, 17–19, 26
Mexico, 17, 37

Newfoundland, 54, 56–57, 59, 67
Niña, 6

Ocean Sea, 5, 8

Parcheesi, 33
Peru, 18, 37
Pinta, 6
pottery
   Asian, 29–30, 33, 36
   New World, 28–30, 33

Rhode Island coal, 59–60

sagas, defined, 39
San Salvador, 11
Santa Maria, 6
Siberia and land bridge, 20–21

Skraelings, 60
   defined, 47
   fights with Vikings, 47, 50
   identity of, 57, 59
Spain, 6, 11
Svein, king of the Danes, 51

Thorgilsson, Ari, 51

Vikings
   base on Vinland, 44–45, 54,
     56–57
   defined, 38
   discovery and settlement of
     Greenland, 42
   discovery and settlement of
     Iceland, 39–40
   voyages to Vinland, 44–45, 47,
     50
Vinland, 38
   base on, 44–45, 54, 56–57
   described, 45
   identification of, 53–54, 57,
     59–60
   known in Europe, 51
   naming of, 45
   voyages to, 44–45, 47, 50, 60

Woodland. *See* Markland.